Praise for *Begi*

M000191291

"With warmth and encouragement, Paul Boynton places you and your goals front and center. Read this little gem, get excited, and get going!"

– Joan Lunden

"Paul Boynton's *Begin with Yes* is a manifesto that navigates you through all the stop-signs we face on this journey called 'life.' I'm sending Boynton's book to all my Hollywood friends with the following inscription: You can't end with 'Yes' unless you learn how to begin with it."

– Scott Prisand, Founding Partner
Corner Store Entertainment

"The timing of this book couldn't be more ideal. We're living in a world in which our systems are changing, dissolving or flat-out falling apart, and we feel increasingly stressed under the pressure to balance life, families and careers. We seem to be yearning to get back to a sense of balance, harmony and spiritual equilibrium. *Begin with Yes* is essential reading for those searching to get back to basics – back to balance, harmony and spiritual equilibrium."

– Tshidi Manye, "Rafiki"
Broadway's *The Lion King*

"This book works, as it upends the status quo – and it's fun and it's easy. Simple to read, yet not simplistic. Forget about positive thinking. Ask yourself the right questions, then begin. Paul Boynton makes you want to get up and get going – after your dreams."

– Lesley Valdes, Critic-at-Large, WRTI – FM
and former critic, Philadelphia Inquirer
and San Jose Mercury News

"I keep a copy of this wonderful book in my salon to share with my clients. Many of us live by the Law of Attraction and we know that 'thoughts become things.' *Begin with Yes* by Paul Boynton takes the Law of Attraction one important action step further. Paul gives us a fool-proof way to renew, refresh and begin. All with a one small action word: *yes*. It's how I have always tried to live my life, and it's a beautiful thing."

– Roberto Novo
Roberto Novo Salons, New York and Buenos Aires

"What an inspiring read. I had been dealing with several business obstacles and this book just re-invigorated my positive nature to not let anything get in the way of getting the job done! *Begin with Yes* is a timeless book that has re-affirmed my belief that a positive attitude kick-started with positive actions can overcome any challenge."

– Paul Fox, Co-Founder
EYE Q, Boston, Massachusetts

"You won't want to say 'no' to the ideas in *Begin with Yes*. Life happens in the course of thousands of decisions made moment to moment, large and small. *Begin with Yes* is an inspirational and practical guide to changing the course of your life, with a simple word: Yes!"

– Tom Viola, Executive Director
Broadway Cares / Equity Fights AIDS

"Find power through actions? Dream impossibly and act realistically? Accept change? Paul Boynton shows how a few thousand tiny "yes" responses add up to one giant "Oh yeah, baby!""

– Alice Ripley
Tony Award Winner

ISBN-13: 978-0-9981718-3-8

Published by: Toby Dog Media

FIRST EDITION

Cover design: Craig A. Hart
www.craigahart.com

Photography: Brian Hutchison
www.bhutch3.com

Book design and layout: Dave Bastien
www.gooberly.com

BEGIN WITH YES

A Short Conversation That Will Change Your Life Forever

By Paul S. Boynton

For Susan Boynton, and her enlightened and loving "Falls Island" soul. You, quite simply, are the most beautiful woman I have ever met and you will forever warm my heart and the world with your generous and gentle spirit.

Foreword

I recently discovered this amazing little book through a friend who shared *Begin with Yes* with me. Reading it, I knew almost instantly why this small book has become such a phenomenon! *Begin with Yes* is so much more than just an inspirational book, and it's very much in line with my fundamental life's philosophy of opening your heart and mind and embracing change.

This small gem of a book is now celebrating its 10th anniversary and I can truly see why millions of people all over the planet have responded to its invitation to hope again, to believe in one's dreams again, and most importantly, to believe in oneself again.

Part of the book's charm and power comes from its simple, yet profound conversational style. The author, Paul Boynton, was trained as a therapist, thus, the message is kind, loving, and grounded in reality. It's a conversation that gently acknowledges that an authentic and honest life brings both pain and joy, and clouds and sunshine. It's also a reminder that despite challenging times, once we embrace change we are more resilient than we may realize and we can access our passions and purpose more easily than we think.

Although I have called this a small book because it's easy to read and understand, it's actually a big book because of its open-hearted message that holds a deep respect for our collective journey. It's the kind of book you'll want to share with your family and friends and keep by your bedside. It's the kind of book that will actually change your life!

Happy anniversary *Begin with Yes*. I'm so glad we met!

Love,
Jane Seymour

Introduction

When I first wrote *Begin with Yes* ten years ago, I thought it was a self-help book that would encourage and inspire people to reclaim their dreams and make good things happen in their lives. The writing came easier than I expected and seemed to flow from my heart and mind as if I was engaged in an important and deep conversation with a dear friend.

As it turned out, this "conversation" was as much for me as it was for any potential readers. And although my intention was to help others to grow, deepen and improve their lives, I discovered that I was actually changing my own life as well.

What I thought was a little self-help book turned out to be a big deal for a lot of people. The simple philosophy of how to take small steps that lead to big accomplishments resonated with so many people that it evolved into a community of 2 million friends! And since you are now part of that community, I believe you deserve to know something else about this small book.

Although common sense suggests that the words that I wrote and the conversation we shared came from within, I now know that they actually came through me as much as they came from me.

At first, I hesitated to share this thought as I prepared the 10th Anniversary Edition of *Begin with Yes* because I knew that it might sound a bit too abstract for some, or suggest that I had a special access to a source that I didn't and still don't really understand. What I *do* understand is that when I put my trust in the universe to provide the insight I need, it always appears. This trust lets me 'begin' even when I might not feel like I have everything figured out. I believe the access is there for me, but it's there for you too. It's something we all share.

I set aside my hesitation because I realized the amazing *Begin with Yes* Facebook Community, with millions of folks from all over the world, would understand, or at the very least, gently forgive me for this revelation. I knew that you'd get that the words I wrote were not just about a shared thought, but also about a shared journey. I also knew that I'm attempting to describe with words a mystery we can only grasp with our hearts.

So, as I get ready to send this 10th Anniversary Edition to the printers, I want you to know how much I appreciate your love, support and generosity, and your kind words, encouragement and prayers. I believe with all my heart that we've been drawn together on purpose to support each other as we create and live the best, most meaningful, and most authentic lives we possibly can.

I'm so grateful that you're part of the *Begin with Yes* family and so grateful that we're taking this amazing journey together, because even though we can't possibly see all the twists and turns ahead, we know we are not alone.

With gratitude, respect, admiration and love,

Paul

There's a wonderful bit of Chinese wisdom that asks, "When is the best time to plant a tree?" The answer is "20 years ago, but the next best time is right now." If you're reading these words, I am convinced they were meant for you, and our timing is perfect.

Begin with Yes

Preface

If you're anything like me and have goals to achieve, ideas to advance, and problems to solve, *Begin with Yes* will have you moving quickly forward, having fun with the process, and getting things done in ways you never imagined possible.

Begin with Yes is an exciting new way to approach life, but be warned: it challenges the status quo and is completely contrary to just about everything you've been taught about success, solutions, personal motivation, and the power of positive thinking.

As a CEO, corporate consultant, motivational speaker, and professional and personal coach, I have had the privilege of working with many, many people who have wanted to improve their lives, move beyond the professional and personal challenges that were holding them back, and make good things happen. Together we have learned a great deal and have made great strides forward.

And through my work, I made one very important discovery that remarkably and powerfully changed my life and became the core of *Begin with Yes*: Contrary to what we've been taught, the secret to a good life is not about having a positive attitude; it's about taking positive actions. In fact, — and this may surprise you — *Begin with Yes* works with or without a positive attitude.

I wrote this book to share the three primary *Begin with Yes* strategies in a way that's easy to understand and easy to implement. *Begin with Yes* is all about asking the right questions, taking the right actions, and finally, navigating safely through obstacles and roadblocks. The book's Q & A format allows a conversation to unfold between us, one that anticipates what you might ask and uses plenty of real-life examples to show you the way. It mimics the counseling, coaching, and presentations I've done over the years since they in essence have flowed like intimate chats about personal change.

Now I will confess that I've always been an optimistic guy, but before *Begin with Yes*, I never fully understood the power of optimism. Nor had I been able to translate my basic positive nature into actions that moved me through difficult times or opened doors that would allow me to achieve the many dreams I had.

That all changed during a very difficult professional and personal dry spell, when *Begin with Yes* really fell into place for me. I was moving toward some painful and significant personal life changes and also treading water in a long-term job that had once been exciting and fun, but was now a "holding place" where I was underperforming and underappreciated. Slowly it dawned on me that some significant changes were needed, and I began to realize that if things were going to shift, I was the one who had to do the shifting.

That important insight led to a deliberate change in my approach to problems and opportunities, and with that change, the *Begin with Yes* principles quickly emerged. As I implemented the simple tools and techniques I had developed, my personal and professional life began to blossom in unexpected and wonderful ways. And that's what I want for you, too.

Begin with Yes is both an approach to life and a simple, natural way to retrain your mind to think in an open, creative way that energizes and engages your problem-solving capacity. It teaches you how to redirect your thoughts in ways that liberate your creativity, get you moving, and keep you moving in positive, productive ways. With *Begin with Yes,* you'll be creating a new mindset that will improve performance and allow you to more fully embrace and finally enjoy your life and the wonderful opportunities that surround you.

When you face life with a *Begin with Yes* spirit, you'll actually be creating positive energy and hope, not just for yourself, but also for the other people in your life. And the positive energy you create will help you get things done, make good things happen, and help you move more easily through difficult and challenging times.

Let's Begin

People sure are stressed. We're working harder and moving faster. We're multi-tasking, answering cell phones, sending emails, tweeting on Twitter, and making friends with people we'll never meet or even truly know on Internet sites that are robbing us of our time, while giving very little back in true reward or value.

We're bombarded with news, most of it depressing, and overwhelmed with schedules that are impossible to keep. We wake up early with an endless list of things to do, and we get to bed late, tossing and turning as we mentally prepare our list for tomorrow. It's no secret that our effectiveness and efficiency suffers as life becomes more complicated. And as the pressure mounts, most of us also find that we have fewer moments of happiness, less time for our family and friends, and little or no time for ourselves and our dreams.

I know how hurried life feels because I feel it too. With all that's going on, we hardly have time to breathe, much less time to read another book. But stay with me for a bit. *Begin with Yes* principles can and will move you quickly and gently into calmer waters where you can manage your life and responsibilities and still have time and energy for family and friends. Even more importantly, you'll discover ways to dust off a dream or two and embrace life in ways you never imagined possible.

Begin with Yes is an intentionally short book with a simple, easy to understand, message of hope and a clear, easy to follow pathway to a more focused, productive, and exhilarating life. I am convinced the *Begin with Yes* approach will work for you just as it has worked for me and for so many of the people I have had the privilege to coach. I know things can be better, life can be easier, and your dreams can still come true.

One of my favorite *Begin with Yes* stories is about my good friend, Broadway composer Mark Schoenfeld. At 57, he was virtually homeless with no show business experience or connections and not a dime in his bank account. All he had was a boom box with some beautiful songs he had written and a remarkable story that he believed was destined to become a Broadway musical.

When I first met Mark, I'll admit that I thought his hopeful and steadfast belief that he'd get his show to Broadway was incredibly naïve. But guess what? He proved me and everyone else wrong when *Brooklyn The Musical* opened on Broadway a few years ago. Want to know how he made that happen? He relentlessly searched for "yes" opportunities. Mark lived, slept, and breathed his passion and stayed with it until he convinced many others not only to believe in his story, but also to invest financially and artistically in a dream that he knew just had to come true.

Many of his "yes" opportunities came about because Mark was (and still is) a master networker. If he identified someone he thought could help him, he began a relentless search for someone who knew someone who knew someone who could make the connection happen. He practiced the law of six degrees of separation and he proved it true. He also developed a captivating pitch that was attention getting and effective. I would guess that he spent as much time fine-tuning the pitch as he did writing the musical. Then, when he did get someone to listen, he would play every character in the musical. It didn't matter that he has what he calls "the worst voice you ever heard"; he would sing with so much passion that potential investors were enthralled, with many becoming convinced that the show would be a smart investment.

Mark was also bold: he did not hesitate to ask for help and was not afraid to ask for money! He didn't let rejection slow him down. When he got a "no thanks" he just moved to the next person on his list. And this focused action didn't stop when the show opened on Broadway. Mark, finally a successful playwright and composer, would go to the half-price ticket line in Times Square and chat with people standing in line to buy tickets. He'd tell them his story, urge them to buy tickets to his show, and then give them his cell phone number, asking them to call afterwards to tell him what they thought. Then every night before and after the show he was outside the theatre meeting people, generating loyalty through relationships, and creating his own "word of mouth" buzz. He was not shy about making things happen and because of that things did happen!

One of the songs from Brooklyn, "Once Upon a Time," has become a standard audition piece for professional actors in New York City and throughout the world. Search it out on YouTube and you'll find many hopefuls singing Mark's song, but more importantly you'll see the power a *Begin with Yes* approach to life can have.

Mark's story is fairly dramatic, but I've seen *Begin with Yes* work for all kinds of people in all kinds of situations: new college graduates looking for a first job; people recently laid off looking for a major career change; artists trying to find gallery exposure; business leaders hoping to improve morale at their workplace; parents and teachers trying to solve a student's problem; an actor needing to nail an audition; a single person looking for a meaningful date; entrepreneurs who have a great idea but don't know what to do with it; social workers looking for shelter for a client; trapeze artists needing to find a circus. My point here is that *Begin with Yes* will work for everyone, but most importantly, it will work for you.

Incidentally, a good friend and colleague once joked that during her college years, "beginning with yes" got her into a lot of trouble. We laughed about that and realized that, as simple as it sounds, *Begin with Yes* does need a bit of explaining.

In the pages ahead, I will describe the *Begin with Yes* approach to life and show you how to adopt it for yourself. I will also be sharing more of my story and the inspiring stories of friends, business associates, and people I have coached. This short book, or rather conversation, reflects what I've learned in my own *Begin with Yes* journey and answers the questions people most frequently ask as they are beginning to explore making this shift in their own lives.

I'm ready and I do kind of like the sound of "Begin with Yes." It sounds a bit like "The Power of Positive Thinking" repackaged. I'm looking forward to learning exactly how Begin with Yes works and how it will impact my life.

If you've ever learned to play a musical instrument, then this illustration of how *Begin with Yes* works will strike a chord with you. Most of us couldn't sit down at a piano and play Beethoven without in-depth instruction, sheet music, and lots of practice. It's like that with life. *Begin with Yes* is an easy to understand process with some simple-to-use tools that will help you learn how to play your life, like a concert pianist plays a beautiful concerto.

As we get started, it's important to note that having an optimistic attitude doesn't hurt and does make things a little easier, BUT it isn't necessary. The emphasis of the *Begin with Yes* approach is on "Begin," and the "Yes" outlook follows. *Begin with Yes* is about action. By taking action we often find our optimism or enhance it. We don't need to ask, "How do I feel?" We need to ask, "What can I do?"

Having said that, I am a great proponent of seeing the glass as half full. So even if that doesn't come naturally to you, I hope you'll be willing to give it a try. If you do, you'll discover that having high hopes is definitely not an idealistic, naïve approach to life. Having high hopes is actually a down-to-earth, common sense approach to making good things happen and facing challenges head on.

A *Begin with Yes* approach also requires a little elbow grease and discipline. *The Little Engine That Could* is not a classic children's story because it's cute. It's a classic children's story because it's true. A sense of hope combined with hard work and tenacity always delivers results. So roll up those sleeves and let's see what problems you can solve, what opportunities you can uncover, and what changes and dreams you can set in motion.

And by the way, you were right when you asked about its similarity to Norman Vincent Peale's successful and motivating book. *Begin with Yes* and *The Power of Positive Thinking* do have a lot in common, but there's a fundamental distinction: they're built on different philosophies. Each is valid, and their effectiveness simply depends on which approach feels more natural to someone.

Peale's book helps the reader to cultivate a more hopeful attitude, but that can seem like an impossible task to some people. *Begin with Yes* proposes an easy, step-by-step method that proves just how accessible, how very *possible*, personal change can be. The *Begin with Yes* approach moves you into a truly authentic, experienced-based, positive mindset; it's less about a positive attitude than about positive actions. In other words, you change your behavior first and the positive thinking takes care of itself.

Are you saying I don't need to have a positive attitude to practice a Begin with Yes approach to life?

You've got it – that's exactly what I am saying. *Begin with Yes* is action-oriented rather than attitude, feeling, or thought-based. It works with or without a positive attitude already in place. I'll be talking more about the importance of attitude later on, but for now, let's stay action-focused and grounded in real life. In other words, even if you typically have a half-empty style, *Begin with Yes* can work for you. If on the other hand you already are an optimistic person, you'll learn how to focus all that good energy and more effectively harness your power.

Optimism at its best is much different from a "head in the sand" mentality. I know life is not always easy, and sometimes the challenges we face can feel overwhelming and frightening. We all struggle and we all know disappointment and despair. Believe me when I say I am not discounting or minimizing your pain. In fact, *Begin with Yes* works because it's firmly grounded in the difficult realities and challenges we all face.

You'll see that, as our conversation unfolds, we will be focused on some of the shared ups and downs of life. I know they're real, and I know they impact your life, just as they have and will continue to impact mine.

*I am beginning to see how **Begin with Yes** is different from just having positive thoughts, but I am still a little skeptical about being able to maintain an optimistic view during difficult times. How do you reconcile the two?*

You're right, difficult times do ebb and flow, and some times are definitely more challenging than others. During difficult times people often ask, "Is it realistic or even practical to have a positive outlook now?"

I understand and appreciate that question and believe that during challenging times we need *Begin with Yes* more than ever, But at the same time, our optimism must be grounded and respectful of the hard realities all of us face. Let me speak a little bit more about this important topic.

As I said earlier, I am a big believer in reality, and I understand the importance of keeping one foot on the ground. Reality can, however, be a tricky concept. First of all, our individual views (our realities), which we sometimes represent as the way things are, are really just the way things seem to be to us at the moment. In other words, what's real is often less about fact and more about the spin or interpretation we place on what we see happening to us and around us. Some people react to a hot, humid 90 degree day as the perfect beach day. Other people react to the very same weather as tiring, stifling, and downright unpleasant. Who's right? What's real?

We know from experience that moment by moment things change, and our realities are constantly shifting. I'd be willing to bet that some days are "beach days" for you but there are other days where the very same heat is nearly unbearable. That's why the "grounded in reality" concept is so essential to talk about.

How do we stay grounded with a *Begin with Yes* approach and still deal with the reality shifts that always seem to be happening?

Here's an example that might help: Today is a good day if we've had a good night's sleep, our kids have new school clothes and we're not worried about our credit card bills or what it costs to fill up the car with gas. Today is *not* such a good day if we woke up with a toothache, couldn't find the car keys, and a friend bailed out on childcare assistance when we truly counted on him. Reality shifts are inevitable, but a *Begin with Yes* outlook can help you stay focused and grounded no matter what kind of day you seem to be having.

It's easier to steer a boat in calm waters just as it's easier to be optimistic when things are going well. On the good days, *Begin with Yes* makes perfect sense and keeps things moving at a brisk and positive pace. But on a bad day, a well-meaning slogan just isn't enough. On those not-so-good days we need to respect our realities, be gentle with ourselves, and be gentle with the people around us. Being gentle, however, does not mean we abandon the *Begin with Yes* approach. In fact, on those bad days, we actually need *Begin with Yes* even more.

When I am having a bad day, first of all, I play some uplifting music on my iPod. Then I gravitate to others whose current realities may be a bit brighter than mine. (It's amazing how being around positive people can lift us to a better place.) Third, I begin asking a lot of questions like: "What can I do to make this easier? What can I do to make things go more smoothly? What do I need to do to feel better?" When I ask these questions, I almost always get a surprising and helpful answer or two that clearly suggest an action. Finally, I take action.

For instance, the other day I was dealing with a personal disappointment and feeling a bit wounded and awkward about a social encounter that had not gone well. I spoke to my daughter Molly about what had happened and then headed out to get a waffle with some real maple syrup. A bit later Molly called my mobile phone to see if I wanted to go to a funny movie later that night. I could have said, "no" and stayed stuck in an uncomfortable place, but instead I thought "yes" and said "sure." The answer to the question, what could I do to feel better? uncovered several small steps (reaching out to someone helpful, a waffle with real maple syrup, and making plans to see a funny movie), and I took them. Gradually the funk I was in began to fade.

But what if you feel that you have very few positive people in your life? If that's your situation, it will slow you down, but what it means is that bringing more positive people into your life needs to become one of the first things you attend to. You might have heard about the "Law of Attraction," a principle centered on the belief that thoughts and feelings are energy, and that like attracts like. That is, positive thoughts and feelings draw positive people and events into your life, and similarly, negative thoughts and feelings attract more negativity. There's no judgment involved; it's just the way energy works. So if you are lacking positive people in your life, the Law of Attraction suggests that some personal shifts might also be in order.

In general there are plenty of positive people around. It's like trying to find a good fishing pond — you just have to ask around a bit. I have found that people who are engaged in life, who are making things happen, people who like their work or have a hobby that excites them often have a more positive outlook. So the question is, who do you know who is engaged with life? Then, the next question (which will lead to an action) is, how can you meet them? All it takes is connecting with one positive person. When you find him or her, I promise there will be other positive people nearby. There is no pond with only one fish.

Begin with Yes is based on the premise that there are always answers to be found and when we find them, we'll uncover actions that will move us forward. This is important and is worth repeating. We ask ourselves questions to uncover actions, and we know as we take these actions that our reality will begin to shift and we will find ourselves moving toward a better place. Let's use that toothache to better understand this principle.

Begin with Yes is really more about positive actions than about positive thoughts or feelings. It requires us to acknowledge reality, (our tooth really does hurt) but then teaches us to focus less on the pain (that toothache) and more on the solutions (a couple of aspirin and a trip to the dentist). It doesn't pretend the toothache isn't real, but propels us into action so that we can deal with the pain and get to a better place.

I hope you fully understand that I have toothaches and down moments and negative thoughts just like the rest of the world. I am not a robotic optimist or inexperienced in disappointments, heartbreak, setbacks, and pain. But I have learned this: The sooner I can shift into action, the better off things become and the sooner I begin to feel better.

That is sounding hopeful and encouraging, but it's also sounding a bit too easy or too good to be true. I can see how this would work for those little problems but what about the really big ones – like an unhappy marriage?

Begin with Yes is good and is true, but sometimes the ideas are misunderstood. Again, I do not want to minimize the gravity of some of the issues we face. An unhappy marriage is a serious and complex reality and a *Begin with Yes* approach to facing it will invite all kinds of self-directed questions and all kinds of essential soul-saving, subsequent actions.

The process that will be set in motion to deal with a troubled marriage will naturally be much more complex with many more steps then the minor social upset I spoke of earlier. But big or small, the process is the same. Ask the questions, note the actions suggested, and begin taking small steps in the right direction.

The ultimate end point for an unhappy marriage could run the gamut from re-discovering the joy in the relationship to, at the other extreme, a decision to end things and move on. As difficult as a "moving on" experience might sound, the alternative is staying stuck in a bad situation, and that just doesn't make sense.

Another key point worth noting is that *Begin with Yes* is not just about challenges; it's also about opportunities and dreams. Perhaps you've been thinking about going back to school or learning to play the piano or lacing up those rollerblades in the attic. Maybe you have a novel to write, an apartment to rent, or a business to start. A *Begin with Yes* approach to opportunities is equally important, and when you begin, you'll be adding some real excitement to your life. Again the process is a series of questions followed by subsequent manageable steps or actions, then more questions and more actions, and so on and so on.

Remember, whether you use *Begin with Yes* for big challenges or little ones, big opportunities or smaller ones, the process is the same and the results are positively predictable. I am not promising you a perfect life, or even a perfect day. But I can promise you this: If you *Begin with Yes*, your life is absolutely going to change. Things are going to get more hopeful, and you will begin moving in positive directions. And as your life changes, I am also convinced that you will find a positive outlook emerging or an already positive outlook enhanced.

I guess I must have a few issues or dreams kicking around, but I'm having a hard time articulating them or even knowing exactly what I'd like to have happen in my life.

It's funny, most people say that, but deep down they really do know. The other day I saw a funny bumper sticker that asked: "What do you know that you're not letting yourself see?" It reminded me of many of my own breakthrough moments and also of a recent coaching session with an executive confused about her future career goals. She kept telling me how much she loved her current job and work environment, but I wasn't convinced. So, I pushed a bit by asking her to tell me the absolute, uncensored truth about why she stayed in her current position. She was actually stunned by her own answer: "Job security." She didn't really love her job at all; she was just afraid to give up the security of work she's been doing for years. With that awareness we were able to begin having productive conversations about her future goals.

If you and I were in a coaching relationship or just having a cup of coffee together, I know we would easily discover some of the changes you'd like to see happen. So get that cup of coffee or tea, relax, and try this quick exercise. Let's uncover a challenge or two and also some of your hopes, dreams and desires that have been put on the back burner.

Seriously, put this book down and get a blank sheet of paper and draw a line down the middle. On the left side, make a list of what you'd like to see happen in your personal life, your work life, and if you're so inclined, your spiritual or inner life, too. Think big and don't be afraid to include things that don't seem practical or even possible. We're talking about your heart's desires. Have fun and let me know when you're through.

All right, my list is done. So how does that translate into Begin with Yes actions that will get things started?

Good work! I'm glad you're already engaged and I can assure you we're already making progress. Go back to the list of what you'd like to see happen in your life and ask yourself: "What is one small action I could take today that would move me, ever so slightly, closer toward my goal or closer to a problem resolution?"

Use the right side of your paper to record these notes. If you truly can't think of at least one action step, ask a friend to help you. And if that doesn't work, email me and I will do my best to help you.

Here are some examples from the lists of a few people I have worked with:

Goal: Vivian wants to sell her house and buy a brand new condo in the city.

First step: Get current house appraised and know its true value.

Goal: Kash wants to find a few public venues to display his art.
First step: Have coffee with a friend who is a commercial realtor to brainstorm a list of possibilities.

Goal: Jason wants to stop fighting with his teenage kids.
First step: Call the school guidance counselor for reading recommendations.

Goal: Marie wants to find a corporate training job in a gay-friendly Fortune 500 company near her home in the Northwest.
First step: Get a list of gay-friendly companies in the region.

Goal: Josh wants to move to a warmer climate.
First step: Make a list of locations that would fit the bill.

Goal: Rachel wants to make a CD of some songs she's written.

First step: Call a friend in the music industry and get some preliminary "how to" advice.

Hopefully these examples will help you get started. Once you have completed your own list, pick your top goal and take that first simple action step. It's important to put our conversation on hold for just a few minutes and actively have a *Begin with Yes* experience. Move from theory to practice and then celebrate your beginning!

That was easy. When I look at my list there are so many things to work on – things that I want to work on. Should I approach the list one goal at a time?

I understand how you feel and that speaks to the fact that *Begin with Yes* is not about a project, it's about our lives. I realize that what I'm about to advise is contrary to what most of us have been taught, but I believe that it actually makes more sense to focus on many goals and challenges at the same time because that's how exciting lives unfold.

Think of it as if you were preparing a wonderful Italian dinner. While the water boils, you wash the lettuce and slice the tomatoes. The sauce simmers while you set the table and warm the bread. Multi-tasking is essential if the meal is going to come together by the time company arrives.

Of course I am not suggesting that you overwhelm yourself and let things spin out of control, but don't be afraid to set several things in motion. With time you'll discover that goals will evolve or change, with some goals becoming less important while others move to the front burner. There's a natural flow to this, and you can expect your energy and priorities to shift as certain projects take hold.

As you begin, it will be helpful to use a small notebook to track your various ventures. At the top of the first page, list your first goal and under that, your first action step. Then skip a few pages, leaving room for future steps and then record your second goal and so on.

When you begin to think about a goal, you may be tempted to think through multiple action steps, but *Begin with Yes* works best when you let it unfold step by step. True, you should consider all your goals at once, as I've said, but tackle each goal *one action step at a time*. As you take these steps, you will learn new information that will help guide and uncover what needs to happen next. For example: from the appraisal Vivian discovered that her house would be much easier to sell if she finished the downstairs bathroom. Based on this new information, the appropriate next step (fixing the bathroom), which wasn't apparent before, now was.

If you over think the process, you'll slow yourself down and actually create a plan that will become obsolete almost immediately. Take one small, manageable step at a time!

Save room in your notebook for new or emerging goals, and keep it with you as you go about your life. And also know that sometimes goals change or simply no longer seem important. Keep your goals current and make time every day, no matter how busy you are, to check off one or two action steps as completed. As you check off an action, ask yourself, what's next? If you get stuck on a next step, reach out to friends and associates and brainstorm – you'll almost always find a next step. If you can't find one, reach out to new friends and keep trying until the next step is found.

I have had the incredible privilege to informally and formally coach so many people as they have stepped up to the plate and begun to make things happen in their lives. *Begin with Yes* isn't always easy – but it always works. And please don't expect this to always be a smooth or uneventful ride. I will talk about upsets and roadblocks in a bit, but for now remember that you're moving into the unknown, and you can expect a surprise or two along the way. And if things are moving too slowly or you find yourself stuck, by all means look for a formal or informal coach to help motivate, support, and encourage you.

It's your turn up to bat. Take the list you've developed and begin. You'll soon discover that it's actually exciting to have several things unfolding at once. Sure, you will have days when it will feel like very little progress is being made, but I promise you there will be other days when things come together like a 4th of July celebration!

I am ready to start but have an important question to ask: What about the impossible goals on my list? Let's face it, I am never going to be an Olympian. Should I cross the unrealistic ones off the list?

I love the impossible stuff, so please don't take anything off your list just yet. Let me tell you a quick story about one of my impossible dreams, and you'll understand why I encourage you to hang on to those bigger ideas.

A couple of years ago, in an unguarded moment, I told a newspaper reporter that when I was a kid, I wanted to be a trapeze artist. Naturally this ended up highlighted in the story she wrote, and I endured a few days of good-natured jokes about "flying through the air" wearing tights.

Now clearly my trapeze days are behind me. But some of the clues found in that dream have been very helpful, and I'll explain why in a minute. If "Olympian" ended up on your list, you know the drill. Ask a few questions: What about being an Olympian appeals to you? Is it being fit, the competition, the performance aspect, the recognition, or other things? Once you have a few answers, you can begin to consider other avenues and take a few steps that would begin to satisfy the essence of your Olympian dreams.

For me, the trapeze story was about performance, risk taking, and adventure. Once I had some clarity around my motivations, I began searching for a few more practical ways to satisfy those desires. I began telling a few friends that I had an idea for a TV show. As I talked with people, the idea evolved, and the logical fit between my public speaking, my personal philosophy, my coaching practice, and a possible TV show became apparent. Then I had the good fortune to run into the director of a local TV station at a meeting with an alderman from our community. As the director and I talked, the perfect opening occurred, and she actually asked me if I had any ideas for a new television show. Did I ever! Very quickly things began to fall into place, and soon I had a weekly *Begin with Yes* TV talk show which is taped live (plenty of risk there) and that surely meets some of my performance and adventure needs! I am having a great time with it, and every so often it actually does feel like I'm flying through air.

When I look at the list I just created, it sounds like you're asking me to make some big changes.

You're right, there are a few changes ahead. But with all due respect, I am not really the one asking; you are. And furthermore, I suspect it's something you've wanted to do for a while. Moving forward will be a lot easier if you're willing to let go of a few self-limiting beliefs and adopt the *Begin with Yes* approach. Here's how.

I have discovered that optimism is not innate; it's really a choice. Many people think that being an optimist or a pessimist is just how people are; I don't buy that. What I do believe is that most people have learned a way of responding to situations and opportunities around them and that that learned approach has simply become a habit.

The two most common responses to challenges and opportunities are those that begin with "No" and those that begin with "Yes." People who typically begin with "No" shut themselves down before they ever get started. However, people who begin with "Yes" stay open to possibilities and create a creative and intellectual environment where ideas and solutions can be found. Naturally, when ideas and solutions are discovered and then followed by actions, the good lives we've been talking about are much more likely to begin happening.

That's why it's important for you to find within yourself the person who begins with "Yes." Let me be clear. I'm absolutely not asking you to become someone different, I am simply asking you to uncover the authentic *Begin with Yes* person already there. And remember, it really doesn't matter how optimistic or how pessimistic you've always been. Starting right now, it's all about the questions, choices, and actions you'll make moving forward.

Anaïs Nin once said: "We don't see things as they are, we see things as we are." She's right. We each create or choose our own reality based upon past experiences and early learning. What we have labeled as real is often just a choice we've made or a reality we've chosen.

Asking yourself questions, making different choices, and choosing "better" realities is actually a skill that you can learn. Once you've mastered it, it will become second nature, and you will eventually *Begin with Yes* naturally, without thinking much about it.

Of course a new approach takes practice, but what doesn't? You've had years of practice saying "No." "No, I can't jump rope." "No, I can't do math." "No, I can't play Scrabble." "No, I can't apply for that job." "No, I can't play the violin." So don't be surprised that beginning with "Yes" feels a little strange at first, because it is — at first. But here's a promise: With practice, "Yes" will eventually become second nature, and in time, "Yes" will become your new way of being and your new first response. As my partner often reminds me, "Practice makes person."

I am remembering your friend who got into a lot of trouble saying yes... am I supposed to say yes to everything?

This may be one of the most important questions you could ask, and it bothers me to have to say it, but the answer is no. Saying "yes"" is about openness to questions and a search for actions rather than a simple, automated response to every situation or opportunity that comes along.

The other day, for example, my grandson Andrew tried to set me up by asking me if I'd buy him a new computer. Fortunately, I was clever enough not to use the "No" word and actually used his trick question as a teaching moment to clarify what *Begin with Yes* really meant. I told him, "If you really want a new computer, I will help you think of things you could do to make that happen." I didn't promise a quick fix, and the obvious suggestion to work and save money wasn't the answer he was hoping for. But I think he got the point. Technically, I was saying "no" to a handout but more importantly, I was saying an encouraging "yes" to the concept of making something happen.

In other situations you may need to say "no thanks" to a late dinner and "yes" to a good night's sleep before an important early morning business meeting. Or you may need to say "No, I won't marry you" while saying "yes" to your right and need to make a heartfelt and wise decision about whom to marry.

OK, I'm ready to give all this a try and I understand it will require a little effort. How exactly do I begin?

It's really pretty simple. Begin by paying attention to how often you say "no." In this case, "no" can be an absolute "no" or a softer, turning away from possibility or opportunity kind of "no."

As you begin to pay attention to the times you say "no," begin to imagine more open "yes" responses. For example, instead of saying "no, I can't play the violin," (because that's real...you can't), say, "Yes I could learn to play the violin if I found a teacher and rented an instrument." Because that's true too: you could. It's really about learning to shift how you view the world. Remember, the "no" approach stops you in your tracks. The *Begin with Yes* approach will have you playing the violin by your next birthday! It's all about shifting your vantage point, or outlook, and it's about choosing realities that work better for you.

Here's another example of how you can use any moment or situation to practice. Imagine you're out to dinner with friends at a nice restaurant — great décor, music, ambiance, but something's not right — and it's your server. She's aloof, slow, and not very helpful; she seems preoccupied and indifferent. You begin to feel annoyed and maybe even a little angry. You might say to your friend, "The service is terrible! This server is a loser!" And you begin to think about how much you'll leave for a tip – like maybe not even enough to buy a gallon of milk.

Now here's your chance to practice shifting. Imagine your server is a single mom. This is actually her second job. She's been on her feet since 6:00 a.m. and won't get done until after 11:00 p.m. Her support payments are two months behind, her daughter is having problems in school, and the rent is late. Christmas is coming, but she's not worried about presents for her kids, she's wondering how she's going to buy a gallon of milk for breakfast tomorrow.

Can you sense a shift? Suddenly your ⸍
You see things differently. Same wom⸍
lousy service, but there's been a shift in your thinking. ⸍⸍
there's a shift in your reality. I suspect now your tip will be
encouraging and generous. The facts haven't changed, but your
reality has. And naturally, as your reality shifts, so do your
feelings, attitudes, and actions.

That's what shifting perspectives is all about. It doesn't always
feel natural or easy. And in fact, sometimes it seems next to
impossible. But with practice, it gets easier, and with lots of
practice, it becomes a way of life.

It sounds like you want me to "make up stories" to make myself feel more positive or hopeful.

Well, with all due respect, that's what most of us do anyway. We are constantly making up stories, so why not make up ones that soften our lives and help us evoke a spirit of compassion for ourselves and the people around us? It's at least worth a try, isn't it?

It's actually beginning to sound like fun, and I am up for giving it a try.

Good for you! But it gets better. Here's another wonderful thing about the *Begin with Yes* approach: When you take positive steps and shift your perspective, you discover how powerful you really are. And who couldn't use a little more power?

Sadly, the truth is that many of us often feel that we don't have enough power. In fact, feeling powerless is probably much more common than feeling powerful.

I learned a very important lesson a while back and that is, just because we feel it, doesn't necessarily make it true. For example, sometimes my granddaughter Gracie is afraid of the dark. (Actually, sometimes I'm afraid of the dark.) Feeling scared is real enough, but just because we're afraid doesn't necessarily mean that there's something in the dark to be afraid of.

It's like that with personal power. Sure, feeling powerless is a real feeling. But just because we don't feel powerful doesn't mean we aren't powerful. In fact, more often than not, the feeling of powerlessness simply means we haven't found our power. When you *Begin with Yes*, you will not only begin to find your power, but you will also begin using it to make good things happen. Think of it in this way: Instead of sitting in the dark complaining about not seeing, stand up, turn on the lights, and get on with your day.

It's a tactic that worked well for Tim, a close friend of mine who was always bemoaning the shortage of good men in his life. He was constantly thinking about a long-term relationship but never seemed to find the kind of guy he wanted to bring home to meet his family. I remember asking him a few questions, and the one that seemed to resonate was this: Where would you most likely meet the kind of man you're looking for?

He didn't even have to think about it: museums, art galleries, and through outdoor activities. From there we brainstormed a bit more and discovered a few potential action steps. He narrowed his options and took the simple steps of signing up to volunteer at the local museum and joining The Appalachian Mountain Club. The last time I spoke with Tim, he was having fun, meeting great people, and even dating a special guy he was bringing home for Thanksgiving.

I like this a lot, but let's be realistic; in many situations we truly are powerless. Clearly not everything is in our control.

I get that, and you are absolutely right. There are a million things outside of our control. But the strategy that works for me, and one I hope you'll be willing to try, is to shift your energy and focus away from what's not in your control and toward the things that are. In other words, stop complaining about all the power you don't have and get smart about all the power you do have.

Incidentally, my experience is that nine out of ten times, (probably ninety-nine out of one hundred times) what's not in our control is everyone else, and what is in our control is ourselves. If you find yourself worrying about or trying to control your partner, family members, or friends, there's a good chance the problem is yours, and at the very least you have some questions to ask yourself. Moving forward, your new focus is to ut what everyone else should be doing and put that energy into making good things happen in your own life. Here's a tip that will change your life: Give up trying to control everyone. Let it go. Trying to control others is annoying (and boring) and it doesn't work. So stop trying.

While I'm at it, here are two other things that don't work: complaining and judging. I've noticed that people who complain all the time or are overly judgmental are typically people who feel pretty powerless. The less power they feel they have, the more they complain or judge. I think that's because when we feel powerless, we feel a need to find scapegoats — people, things, and events to blame. When we feel powerless, we often try and "steal" other people's power by being judgmental (which often comes in the form of putting someone else down) and that just doesn't work.

Has listening to others complain ever inspired or motivated you or added to your day in a positive or helpful way? I think that as you tune in to the complainers in your life and also note how often you find yourself complaining, you'll be inspired to redirect your energy.

I think it's also incredibly important to begin to pay attention to how often we speak in judgmental ways with a judgmental tone in our voice. It's helpful to recognize how harmful all this judging is, not only to the people being judged but also to the one doing the judging. As I see it, when we judge, we are creating negative energy that impacts everyone touched by it.

When you find yourself or others complaining or judging, simply practice redirecting or re-phrasing. The other day I was out for a ride with a friend and saw a newly built house that I didn't like and said, "Look at that ugly house." As soon as I said it, I realized how negative and ridiculous it sounded. Instead I could have said, "Look at that house; it's not my style." With that shift, the conversation would have been about my personal preferences and would have felt less critical and judgmental. Conversations about personal likes and dislikes are an interesting way to get to know someone. Critical or judgmental conversations are just critical and judgmental!

Think of how often we describe a book or movie or dinner or work of art as awful, when what we're really describing is what does not appeal to us. Now one could argue that words don't have that much impact, but I believe our words create our reality. With this in mind, we should choose carefully.

When we connect with our own power, turn on our power switch, then there's no need to blame because there's nothing to blame anyone for. There's no reason to "steal" power because we already have plenty of our own. Remember this the next time you're stuck in a conversation with an overly judgmental, critical, or complaining person. And more importantly, remember it the next time someone else is stuck in that kind of conversation with you.

So how do we find our power switch?

You simply and deliberately shift to a *Begin with Yes* mindset.
That means you begin to ask a few questions and search for
"yes" answers and action steps. When you do, suddenly the
lights go on. What do I mean, exactly? Here are a few examples
of turning on your power switch:

• Call the theatre to see what movies are playing and what time
the shows are

• Make an appointment to have your eyes checked

• Invite a friend over to help you learn to balance your
checkbook

• Offer to take an elderly friend to the mall for a walk

• Get gas for the lawnmower

• Shut the TV off and bake some brownies

I know some of these examples seem small and almost too easy, but that's the point. If you're doing something, you're doing something. If it's getting you closer to a goal or solving a problem, or just making you feel better, it's power!

Finding our power when we're overwhelmed, confused, or depressed requires us to do something even when we don't want to or don't feel we can. We have all been there, and taking action is the only way out. We may not be able to clean the entire house but we can clean out one kitchen drawer. We may not be able to find a new job but we can make a list of the kinds of jobs that might appeal to us.

The power switch is activated by any small action. Taking an action, no matter how small, sets things in motion, and motion, no matter how small, is power. As you exercise your power, you'll likely discover that the next step is a bit easier. Once the drawer is organized, taking out the trash seems more manageable. Once the trash is gone, it might make sense to sweep the floor and empty the dishwasher. With *Begin with Yes*, the house gets cleaned because you started with the kitcnen drawer.

Remember you don't find your power and then take action. You find your power by taking actions. Gradually accessing your power will feel more and more natural, and you'll begin to feel more energized and able to make good things happen.

Many great teachers have taught, "You are what you think." Think pessimistic, powerless, "No" thoughts, and that's what you are. Think optimistic, powerful, "Yes" thoughts, and that's what you are. When I first began practicing to increase my "Yes" responses, I put *Begin with Yes* index cards everywhere: on my desk at work, the refrigerator, the bedside table, and in my shirt pocket. I needed to constantly remind myself to look for "yes" pathways instead of automatically reverting to the "no" dead ends.

A good friend of mine, Dave Bastien, who founded a wonderful organization called Musicians for a Cause, once shared his observation that the word "Begin" is just as important as the word "Yes." He was absolutely right, and helped me understand that we turn on the power when we simply begin. And to begin, all you need to do is *do something*! Take a step – any step – in the right direction, and the power switch will be activated. Try it. You'll be thanking Dave, too!

Incidentally, Dave is another *Begin with Yes* story. As a high tech executive in a declining business environment, he found himself wondering where his life was heading and searching for his purpose. Music and songwriting had always been his passion, yet he'd let them take a back seat to his job and his life in general.

One day the universe decided it was his turn to be on the outside looking in, and he was laid off. While considering his future, he met with a counselor who helped determine his path with one question: *"What would you be doing with your life if you didn't have any outside responsibilities?"* His answer came without hesitation: "I'd use music to help bring awareness to causes." At that moment he realized he could never go back to the corporate world.

His counselor challenged him to develop a plan, and although he could have taken the easier route and found another job in the corporate world, he said yes to the challenge. It took several years, but he stuck with it until Musicians for a Cause was born.

Saying yes and acknowledging his passion drove Dave to seek out people he thought could offer helpful advice on how to make Musicians for a Cause a viable organization. He always says, "Tell others your dreams; they'll help them come true." When he realized that that advice applied to him too, his own dreams started taking shape.

Hmmm... following his own advice. That brings up a trap many of us fall into: we're great at offering advice to others, but all too often we can't see how to apply the same words of wisdom to our own lives. I'll bet as you're reading this, you're reflecting on your own example, and that's great! Now take that example, apply the *Begin with Yes* principles, and just watch what happens.

I wish I had people in my life like Dave!

Well there's even more good news: Power and optimism attract, actually generate, more power and optimism. When you set "Yes" in motion, don't be surprised when people like Dave, with good energy, suddenly appear and unite to support and maintain your momentum.

Earlier, I talked about the "Law of Attraction." In short, we attract a certain kind of person by being a certain kind of person. Pessimistic people seem to attract pessimistic people, while optimistic people tend to attract optimistic people.

Marianne Williamson, author of *A Return To Love*, took it a step further when she wrote: "You can see the glass half empty, or you can see it half full. You can focus on what's wrong in your life, or you can focus on what's right. But whatever you focus on, you're going to get more of." Marianne is right: half full or half empty is not just an attitude; it's a prognosis. And half full doesn't just attract people. It attracts wonderful opportunities.

If I am beginning to attract more o
people, what about all the other, less positive
people already in my life?

That's an important question, and I'm glad you asked. If you take *Begin with Yes* seriously, there will be many shifts, and some of them will involve family, friends, and business associates that may have been in your life for a very long time.

If you have pessimistic, critical, complaining, powerless people around you, some will be unsettled by your new approach to your life. On the other hand, some of them may be intrigued by your new, hopeful, action-oriented, self-directed style, and they'll grow with you.

Unfortunately, others may decide to move away, which will be sad, but also OK because you will find yourself less willing to spend time with people who bring you down. And finally some people will actually resist *Begin with Yes* (sometimes as if their lives depended on it) and try to bring you back into their "no" comfort zone. When that happens, you're going to need to stay alert, be clear, set some boundaries, avoid trying to control others, and remind yourself that your new approach is just plain better for you and the world.

Change isn't always easy. The kinds of changes you decide to make may lead to some losses, and I don't want to minimize the significance of letting some things go. I am not sure it's even possible to let go without tears, so be gentle with yourself and those around you. When you say yes to your life, also say yes to your feelings and keep things moving in the direction your heart desires.

Let me say a few more words about clarity and boundaries. Often we find ourselves annoyed, frustrated, or even angry with others because we have not been clear about our own boundaries. Some of us (and I put myself in this group) were taught to defer to others in ways that don't really make sense. For example, if you really want to take a photography class, but your boyfriend wants to spend more time with you, it's better to be clear with him about your preference and work on a compromise that allows time for the photography class. Otherwise, not only will you be compromising your dreams but your resentment will also create bad vibes that will not serve the relationship.

Many people have a really difficult time being clear about what they want and need. They think they're being nice, but in reality they're being wimps. Trust me. No one worthy of your time, energy, or love wants a wimp for a friend or lover.

If you find yourself annoyed, frustrated, or angry with someone in your life, there's a very good chance you haven't been clear and haven't set appropriate boundaries. The way to improve the situation is not to get them to change; it's for you to be honest about your needs, hopes, and dreams and then respectfully set boundaries. In other words, tell it like it is: "This is important to me. I want to do this, and if I can't have your support and encouragement, at least don't slow me down."

Much of this will be fairly easy to navigate unless the people in question are really significant people in your life – wives, husbands, partners, lovers, parents, brothers and sisters, best friends, your boss, etc. In these situations, the stakes are much higher and your work a bit tougher. I recommend that as you put more energy into attracting positive people into your life, you also build an "invisible shield" to protect yourself from being influenced by the half-empty people who do or must remain.

Attracting more positive people is your offense. Building the shield is your defense. Activating the shield is really a meditative or mental exercise, and a bit of imagination will come in handy. There are many practices out there, and as you talk with like-minded friends or associates you'll likely discover some self-protective techniques that will work well for you. The "shield" is really just a choice or decision to protect yourself from negativity. Imagining the shield in whatever way works for you will help you actualize the protection.

To activate the invisible shield, ask yourself a few questions whenever "downers" attempt to weigh in. For example: "Is this feedback helping me? Is it motivating or encouraging me? Is it inspiring or moving me closer to my goals?" If the answer to any of these questions is "no," then simply and quickly discount the feedback. If someone you loved wanted you to eat some shrimp even though you hate shellfish and it makes you sick, would you eat the shrimp? Of course not.

In extreme situations, one important question you may need to ask is: "Can I break free from this person's controlling behavior without some outside help?" If the answer is: "Not likely," then the obvious action step is to secure the professional help you need to get through this successfully.

This is beginning to feel more like a way of approaching life or a practical process and less like therapy or self-help. What about people who are depressed, anxious, and fearful, or those who have other kinds of emotional issues to deal with, things that are understandably slowing them down?

This is a question that many people sharing this conversation can relate to. I know because these kinds of issues are part of life and become reality for most of us at one time or another. You're also right to remember that *Begin with Yes* is more about action and not really about therapy at all. Think of it as a reminder or gentle push to keep you moving in the right direction; a deliberate, on point, action-based redirection in response to challenges and opportunities. *Begin with Yes* is not a substitute for therapy or other clinical interventions; still, it can help you deal with some of the painful realities mentioned in your question.

A depressed person can still be a *Begin with Yes* person by acknowledging the pain and asking, "What do I need to do to get to a better place?" The answer might very well be to find a good therapist and begin therapy. That moment of awareness followed by action (scheduling an appointment and beginning a therapeutic process) will be a major "yes" step moving the person in a more hopeful direction.

Remember this, no matter where you start, what challenge you face, or what obstacle you need to work through, *Begin with Yes* is designed to get you moving. I think you will be amazed at how soon you will feel deserving of and start finding wonderful opportunities to enhance your life.

Some days I am just plain under moody, and exhausted. The thought of taking positive action seems almost impossible. What can I do on those days?

Sometimes *Begin with Yes* requires us to take action despite our moods and energy levels, but other times it's more about being gentle and kind to ourselves. The trick is deciding when to push forward and when to be gentle. If the mood or exhaustion happens only occasionally, let gentleness prevail. If it's more chronic, then most likely it requires some sort of action. One good place to start is to explore the reasons behind the chronic condition. We do that by asking questions: For example: "Why am I so tired all the time?" "Do I need to talk to my doctor about these headaches?" "How come I've been so moody lately?" "What could I do to feel less anxious?"

The answers then become guideposts or action indicators. If the answer to the question "Why am I feeling depressed?" is because you've stopped taking your antidepressants, then the action is pretty straightforward: Speak with your doctor and figure out how to get back on track.

You've definitely got my attention, but I hope you'll talk a little more about fear. Sometimes that's my biggest roadblock and I am not sure what to do about it.

What a great question. Fear does get in our way and often stops us in our tracks. There are a few *Begin with Yes* techniques that can help.

I was recently coaching a client who had several goals, but the most pressing was a desire to begin dating again. Karen shared that each time she got close to meeting someone new (or even smiling at a good looking man at the grocery store) she got scared and backed off. As we talked about her fearfulness, we suddenly realized that we were focusing on the wrong thing. Ironically, talking about and dwelling on the fear actually invited more fear in. And the fear was keeping her stuck and not getting her any closer to a new relationship.

As we talked, we began looking instead for Yes-type actions she could set in motion despite her fear. For starters, she decided simply to smile more at everyone. In other words, she thought she'd make smiling a habit. Naturally, this new habit extended to interesting men, and soon not only was she routinely smiling at cute guys but even swapping recipes with attractive bachelors in the grocery store. These changes in behavior happened in spite of the fear, not because she had eliminated it. Had she waited for the fear to disappear before taking a simple action, Karen never would have found herself having so much fun in produce!

In our personal lives, fear is often a choice we make. That's right: as I've said, we can actually choose our feelings, and thankfully we can choose something other than fear. See if this example helps. If I'm hiding behind a tree and I jump out and say "Boo," and you jump, that's a normal reaction. But that feeling of being scared soon passes. That's normal too; no problem. However, if two days later, you're still scared, and you're looking behind every tree, that may be a problem.

Fear in response to something that has happened is a reaction. Fear that lingers is most often a feeling. And in that case, the solution, strange as it may seem, is to just choose another feeling. Choosing another feeling is actually easier than it sounds. Simply take an action that moves you forward despite your fearful feelings, and the fear will begin to dissipate. For example: If the goal of returning to college seems overwhelming or even scary, accept that. Then simply figure out a less scary first step like checking out college websites, and do that. After you do that, the next step might be touring a campus or two. Don't focus on your fear or even what it might be like to be in college. Instead focus on the smaller, more manageable next step.

Now don't get me wrong. There truly are many things to be frightened or worried about: hurricanes, bombs, terrorists, world events, the list goes on and on. And then we all have more personal worries: our jobs, the stock market, kids starting first grade, aging parents, illnesses, retirement plans. I'll be willing to bet that there isn't a person reading this that doesn't have his or her fair share of legitimate things to worry about.

Interestingly enough, I don't think of fear or worry as a negative thing. I actually think of these feelings as more neutral. In truth, they are a normal, unavoidable part of the human experience, and sometimes they're actually helpful. Being afraid of deep water when you don't know how to swim makes a lot of sense, doesn't it? In fact, if you've never worried or felt fear…that would scare me.

But I also know that worry or fear doesn't feel good, gets in the way of actions, and almost always zaps us of our energy. In the end, we need to recognize fear and worry for what they are, and then take a deep breath and choose again. Choosing again is what John McCain wrote about in "In Search of Courage," which appeared in *Fast Company's* December 19, 2007 issue: "Don't let the sensation of fear convince you that you're too weak to have courage. Fear is the opportunity for courage, not proof of cowardice." When we decide to *Begin with Yes*, we're really choosing action over fear. We're saying "yes" instead of "no," and we're doing something instead of nothing!

I'm all for choosing action over fear, and all for attracting wonderful opportunities. But I'm beginning to sense that some of the dreams I have will require a few other people who'd be willing to work with me.

I completely understand. You are about to discover that you have always been surrounded by people who are not only willing to help, but are eager to. You just haven't been looking in the right places.

But before you go looking for people to help you realize your dream, there's something funny you should know. You don't really need to focus on finding people to help you. Rather, you need to focus on finding people who need your help. Booker T. Washington wrote, "If you want to lift yourself up, lift up someone else." I know it sounds counterintuitive, but try it. It's really the only way you can experience this wonderful contradiction, and it always, always works.

And that brings me back to Mark Schoenfeld and his Broadway musical. The first time I heard the music from "Brooklyn," I was struck by the lyrics, "When you change someone's life, you change your own." It sounds so simple, doesn't it? Well, that's because it is.

Changing lives is actually pretty darn easy. In fact, much of the fun and joy of *Begin with Yes* comes from a greater awareness of how we impact others and choosing to make life a little better or easier for the people around us. Talk about amazing power!

Remember the limbo? I had the good fortune of being invited to a party recently and there were lots of people and lots of activities. At one point the disc jockey asked me and another person to grab an end of a bamboo pole and hold it horizontally. When it dawned on me that it was going to be a limbo contest, I realized why he had assumed I'd better be one of the people holding the pole. You know the limbo, right? "Jack be nimble, Jack be quick, Jack go under limbo stick...." He took one look and knew I was no Jack.

Well anyway, the line formed and as the song played, the pole got lower and lower and the line got shorter and shorter. It's a competitive game after all. When there were only about four people left, something very interesting happened. As each person leaned way back — and I do mean WAY BACK — to get under the pole, the person behind them reached out, putting their hands under the limbo dancer's shoulders to support them as they slipped under the pole.

This was a new kind of limbo. Not about winning or losing, but about having fun, meeting the challenge, and helping each other do the impossible.

Sometimes I think life feels like we're doing the limbo. Don't you occasionally wonder just how far you can bend before you fall? And wouldn't it be beautiful and wonderful to know that, as you lean back, there would be a pair of hands waiting to hold you up?

You can make that "something wonderful" happen for someone else by simply saying, "Yes, I can be that pair of hands." And what I've experienced over and over is that when I get in that line, and when I do reach out my hands to help, always, when it's my turn to lean back, there is a pair of hands waiting for me.

I recently heard a wonderful quote attributed to Anne Frank, who surely demonstrated a *Begin with Yes* philosophy. She said: "How wonderful it is that nobody need wait a single moment before starting to improve the world." I am certain that Anne Frank saw the inherent relationship between our desire for a good life for ourselves and our willingness to help others to have these opportunities too.

You sure make it sound easy – almost too easy. Are you suggesting that everything will be perfect?

Let me gently remind you that I said "a good life," not "a perfect life."

No life is perfect; no life is without worries or problems. We have good days and good years, and not so good days and not so good years. Sometimes things unfold easily and perfectly, while at other times they zoom downhill faster than a runaway toboggan.

We have happy, even miraculous moments, and we have our share of painful, out-of-the-blue setbacks and losses, too. We all know a good life is not a life without problems. But we also know that a good life doesn't happen by accident — nor does it happen in isolation.

Very recently I had the pleasure of speaking at an event with Bert Jacobs. If you don't know him, I am sure you know his Life is Good® T-shirts. Bert and his brother John co-founded that company. Ten years ago, they were hawking T-shirts out of their van on the streets of Boston, living on peanut butter and jelly sandwiches; today they're at the helm of an international, multi-million dollar company. How did Bert & John do it? They had a *Begin with Yes* attitude.

Bert absolutely believed he could do it. But he also knew he couldn't do it alone. The story of his success is filled with stories of friends and associates who helped him achieve his goals. Evidence of Bert's outlook can be found in his job title: At his company, CEO stands for "Chief Executive Optimist." And believe me, he practices what he preaches. Let me give you an example.

When I first met with Bert, it was to pitch an idea our management team hoped he'd get involved with. It was a real long shot. He's a busy man, I didn't know him or anyone who knew him, and we had no professional or personal connections that might get his attention. But our team headed to his corporate office in Boston to meet him anyway.

After we did our dog and pony show, and made "our ask," guess what Bert said, right then and there? "Yes, I'll do it." His "yes" led to a keynote speaking engagement at an annual meeting I was responsible for and a generous donation to the nonprofit I ran.

I will always be grateful for Bert's help but even more grateful for the lesson this situation taught me. I learned that after all was said and done, it was my open, hopeful, action-oriented "Yes" approach that got me in front of Bert so these good things could happen. Had I chosen a "no, this will never work" attitude, the story I just told you never would have happened!

It's so inspiring to hear your stories, but I'm grounded enough to know that not everything is going to go exactly as planned. How do I deal with setbacks or disappointments?

That's a great question and you're right to expect your share of temporary roadblocks, disappointments, or setbacks. Also be prepared for a few mistakes along the way. Sometimes these upsets are hard to handle and impossible to understand. At other times what we thought was a curve ball turns out to be a wonderful redirection. Either way, upsets are inevitable and it's worth paying attention to how we respond.

One very common reaction to setbacks or disappointments is to look for someone or something to blame. And whether you look outward and blame others or inward and blame yourself, the outcome is always the same.

When you blame, you become stalled in an unhappy, unproductive time warp and are either temporarily sidelined or permanently derailed.

Another common reaction is remorse. I have worked with many people who have a desire, need, or most likely a habit of literally paying homage to their mistakes and setbacks. It's such a colossal waste to spend precious time living in a world of regrets, second-guessing, and dwelling on whatever upset comes along. The end result is always the same: going nowhere fast.

Now obviously some setbacks are much more significant than others and quiet reflection and thoughtfulness are essential. Facing a major illness or relationship shift is much more significant than getting a bad haircut or being late to a movie. Some of us over-react to little upsets as if they were major catastrophes, while others who face more significant life challenges seem to take things in stride. With the bigger challenges, we mistakenly assume some people are more resilient than others, but that's really not true. We are all resilient. After all, we're still here, aren't we?

By now most of us have figured out that we can't choose a life without problems. Upsets are unavoidable. But we do get to choose how we react to setbacks. We get to choose how much energy we direct at feeling bad or self-critical. And we get to choose how quickly we set those feelings aside and move forward.

We all have our own favorite, nonproductive ways of responding to challenges. And we all need to learn and then practice redirecting our energy in positive, productive directions. When you find yourself facing a disappointment, roadblock, or setback, the remedy is to shift away from feeling bad by asking yourself a very powerful question: "Now what?" By asking that question, you immediately shift into possibility mode, and you'll feel lighter and more hopeful as you uncover and take that next reasonable step.

Remember Vivian, the woman trying to sell her house who discovered during the appraisal that she needed to re-do the bathroom? Well, this was a major setback because she didn't have the money to make the essential home improvements. This upset hit hard and she did stay stuck...for about five minutes. But then she simply shifted into the "what now?" question and came up with some great next steps. Vivian decided to strip the wallpaper and do some paint removal herself. She then bartered with her neighbor's son, a plumber, offering to baby-sit in exchange for plumbing assistance. She then had a yard sale and made enough money to buy new fixtures and — the frosting on the cake — convinced her former husband to paint and put down new floor tile.

Vivian laughs about convincing her ex to do the painting, but more importantly she's proud that she didn't get derailed. As she so often says, "If I can do it, anyone can." And she's right: you can!

I am beginning to feel optimistic about feeling optimistic. On one hand it seems easy, and yet I know there's got to be more to it.

I'm glad that you're feeling optimistic, and to be honest, all things considered, a *Begin with Yes* life is actually pretty easy. I know sometimes people get the idea that *Begin with Yes* is about big mountain-moving actions. But really I'm talking about much smaller, very manageable, minute-by-minute actions. It's not one great big "Yes." It's a thousand little "Yeses" that end up making life-changing things happen.

Think of it this way. If you want to write a novel, at some point, you have to just pull out the pen and paper and write that first sentence. And then the next one, and the next one, and pretty soon, you have a rough draft of chapter one. That's how books get written. That's how it works for Dan Brown, that's how it works for me, and that's how it's going to work for you.

When I first began to direct my optimism and power, it made sense to focus on relatively small things. I took a few friends out for coffee to begin to unravel my career confusion. Then I began to explore what was missing in my current job – journaling about my ideal job criteria. I dug up an outdated copy of my resume and looked around for other more contemporary resume formats that I could replicate. Then I drafted a new resume and bounced it off trusted co-workers and a CEO friend of mine. Suddenly I realized that things had been set in motion and I was no longer standing still. Naturally there were many steps ahead and my dream job didn't just magically appear. But to finally be moving inspired me. One step led to another and that dream job did show up! I learned quickly that when we pay attention to the small things, the big things somehow manage to take care of themselves.

Here's what I suggest: If *Begin with Yes* hasn't been your style, now's your chance. And if you already have a positive, optimistic outlook, turn it up a notch! Turn on that power switch and then use the power to set good things in motion. Start small and stay hopeful. Look for those small opportunities to use your power, and then just watch what happens.

Do you have some more suggestions?

I am really glad you asked. Here are a few more ideas. Smile more; say "I'll be glad to help"; hold open a door for someone; let someone else go first; give an encouraging nod to someone up at bat; offer to help someone shovel snow; bring someone a cup of coffee; share a good laugh; let someone else have the parking space; smile some more. The opportunities are endless, and each one is simple, powerful, and life changing. And these seemingly small actions will add up in unexpected, mountain-moving ways. There's not one person reading these words who doesn't have enough power to do what I'm suggesting.

As Anita Roddick, founder of The Body Shop, said, if you think you're too small to have an impact, try going to bed with a mosquito in the room. Sure, there will always be those darn mountains. I suspect there will be a few we can't even imagine. But forget about the mountains for now. Instead focus your attention on the little things. Write that first sentence, solve that small problem, and change someone's next moment. Even Mount Everest was conquered, one step, one inch at a time. And that's how we'll deal with our mountains too: one positive, optimistic action step at a time.

You know, there may be a few people reading this who would like to prove me wrong, but I hope you'll humor me. How about proving me right? Those of you willing to prove me right will find many good things happening and many challenges resolved. And by the way, there's an added payoff I should mention: happiness.

You mean if I develop a Begin with Yes style, I'll be happy?

In a way, that's exactly what I've discovered. A *Begin with Yes* life is not only a good life, it's a life filled with many more happy moments. Let me remind you of something your heart already knows: You don't find happiness. Happiness finds you. When you *Begin with Yes*, you'll be inviting more positive people and moments into your life. You'll become a bright, beautiful sign that says, "Happiness, this way!"

Here's what I've learned: We meet half-empty and half-full people everywhere we go. We meet people who approach life with a "yes" and a smile, and we meet others who approach life with a "no" and a frown.

At the grocery store. At the gym. At the doctor's office. Half-empty and half-full people are everywhere. And that begs the question, a question that each of us needs to ask: who do we want around us? And then the more important question: who do we want to be? The answers to these two questions will suggest clear and simple actions you can take which will move you in the direction you want to move. I hope that you'll choose *Begin with Yes*.

I've enjoyed this little talk, and I will do my best to hang on to these good thoughts. Are there any last minute reminders to keep in mind?

I've enjoyed this conversation too. I am confident you'll choose the good life you desire and deserve, and I wish you Godspeed on your incredible journey, already underway. Please know that in some cosmic, optimistic way, I will be cheering you on from the sidelines, reminding you to ask the questions, take the actions, and keep moving forward one small step at a time.

Can you imagine me smiling now as I celebrate your tenacity, your sense of hope, and your willingness to bravely move through the challenges and embrace the opportunities ahead? My hat is off to you.

Yes, the stakes are high, but those incredible opportunities are so beautiful. This truly is **your** moment. You have always had the power and now you have the tools. The world awaits. *Begin!*

Begin with Yes: The 10 Principles

1. Begin - The best time to start is now.

2. Have a sense of hopefulness and roll up your sleeves.

3. Expect that Begin with Yes will train your mind to think in an open, creative way and empower your problem-solving capacity.

4. Remember, the secret to a good life is less about having a positive attitude and more about taking positive actions.

5. Ask questions. There are always answers to be found and the answers lead to actions that will move you forward.

6. Keep moving one step at a time. Don't let fear stop you.

7. Find your power by taking action.

8. Focus on finding people you can help, rather than on people to help you.

9. It's not one great big "yes." It's a thousand little "yeses" that make life-changing things happen.

10. Begin.

Author Bio

Paul Boynton is the President & CEO of The Moore Center. He trained as a social worker and therapist and has worked in the nonprofit world his entire career. He has blogged for *The Huffington Post* and *The Good Men's Project* and is the host of *Begin with Yes on Empower Radio*. He is the author of several books including *Begin with* Yes, and currently working on his newest book, *Be Amazing*.

His Facebook community, with 2 million followers, is a source of inspiration for those who are taking steps toward a more meaningful life. You can read more at www.beginwithyes.com or join him on Facebook at www.facebook.com/beginwithyes.

Paul lives in New Hampshire with his partner, Michael, and their lovable Goldendoodle, Toby.

Other books by Paul S. Boynton:

- Begin with Yes – A Short Conversation That Will Change Your Life Forever
- Begin with Yes 21 Day Workbook
- Begin with Yes Action Planner
- Commit – Transform Your Body and Your Life With the Power of Yes
- Begin with Yes – At Work for You
- Beginnings – Daily Meditations
- Begin with Yes – Nighttime Affirmations
- Living with a Dream – Inspirational Musical Compilation
- Begin Within – Guided Meditation CD

Begin with Yes Online

Stay with us! Visit www.beginwithyes.com for the latest *Begin with Yes* insights, stories, news, and events, and join the Begin with Yes Facebook family at www.facebook.com/beginwithyes.

With much love and gratitude to Josh, Rachel, Molly, Jason and Tim. You keep me mostly grounded and always laughing. Thanks for my beautiful grandchildren, Grace, Andrew, Kash and Ty. How lucky can one man be!

And finally to Michael, night after night you lovingly read the manuscript, always reminding me to speak from the heart and keep it real and joyful. I am grateful for all that you do and all that you are.